PRODUCED WITH THE SUPPORT
OF THE TSARSKOYE SELO STATE MUSEUM
PRESERVE THE AMBER ROOM REBORN

Director of the Tsarskoye Selo
Amber Workshop public joint-stock company
Boris Igdalov

General preparation of the publication
Liudmila Khaikina, Alexander Minin
Forewords
Ivan Sautov, Lara Bardovskaya, Boris Igdalov

Text by
Liudmila Khaikina
English translation by
Paul Williams
Design by
Alexander Minin
Photographer
Alexander Minin
Proofreader
Irina Dubrovskaya
Computer typesetting
Olga Dubovaya
Colour correction
Tatyana Krakovskaya, Yekaterina Shumikhina

This publication was made possible
by the financial support of Alfa-Colour Publishers.

The author wishes to express her thanks
for assistance in preparing the illustrations to I.G. Lander,
a member of staff at the National Library of Russia.

Colour separation by the Goland company, St Petersburg

ISBN 5-94795-050-2

THE AMBER ROOM
REBORN

Alfa-Colour Publishers
Saint Petersburg, 2004

Specialists involved in the recreation of the Amber Room

Administration: *N. Chekhovich, Zh. Golubitskaya, V. Gromtsev, N. Yeliseyeva, G. Yemelyanova, T. Zharkova, P. Ivanov, V. Ivakha, B. Igdalov, T. Makarova, A. Marchenko, S. Minina, V. Nikonov, N. Petukhov, B. Podolsky, A. Riikonenen, I. Sautov, M. Trufanova*

Researchers and art historians: *L. Bardovskaya, I. Bott, A. Chernova, N. Chudinova, N. Grigorovich, S. Guliayeva, S. Ivanova, L. Khaikina, G. Khodasevich, M. Kolotov, Z. Kostiasheva, A. Kuchumov, N. Lapina, V. Lemus, V. Lugina, A. Ovsianov, V. Plaude, N. Shavrina, T. Suvorova, N. Tarasova, Yu. Trubinov, Ye. Vinogradova, M. Voronov*

Architects: *N. Ivanov, A. Kedrinsky, G. Khazatsky, V. Khazatsky, M. Kononova, Ye. Korovina, V. Lipatova, N. Lobantseva, Ye. Skryvleva, Ye. Volkova, I. Yarotskaya, M. Yelenevskaya*

Modellers: *Yu. Anokhin, Ye. Anokhina, L. Shvetskaya, V. Zaitseva*

Painters: *I. Alexeyev, Ya. Kazakov, A. Kosokovsky, B. Lebedev, L. Liubimov*

Woodcarvers: *V. Antonov, V. Bogdanov, A. Fedotov, A. Kemnits, A. Kochuyev, V. Kochuyev, V. Kosliuk, Yu. Koslov, V. Larionov, Ye. Ostroumov, V. Pasiukov, V. Petrov, Yu. Savelyev, I. Sharmanov, N. Smirnov, A. Vinogradov, A. Zabrovsky, M Zuyev*

Parquet-layers, joiners: *N. Kudriashov, V. Verigin*

Gilders: *T. Akimova, V. Chekushina, N. Fomicheva, L. Grishchenko, A. Khiyenkina, G. Korneva, T. Lazareva, P. Mai, M. Morozova, N. Ovchinnikova, V. Parkhatskaya, L. Petrova, G. Rozina (Gorbacheva), G. Severina, T. Sizova, N. Vinitskaya, G. Yefremova, M. Zavgorodniaya*

Amber-Carvers: *N. Akhtulov, V. Alimov, A. Bashmakov, N. Belitsky, O. Belov, S. Bobovnikov, G. Budiakov, A. Dogadin, Yu. Fedoriak, L. Filimonov, V. Gundarov, S. Ilyin, V. Karnaukhov, A. Khlebayev, A. Konoplev, A. Kovrikova, N. Mazur, V. Medvedev, V. Mezentsev, V. Miasnikov, V. Mikhailov, V. Mikhnevich, V. Minin, B. Mints, V. Mokhov, O. Murashov, A. Murzov, T. Nechipurenko, V. Novikov, I. Petrishchev, V. Smelov, V. Sudnik, S. Vankov, L. Vilde, R. Voyevodov*

Amber Restoration Artists: *V. Domrachev, S. Ivanov, S. Kaminsky, N. Klochkov, A. Krylov, V. Kurakin, A. Movsesian, N. Petrov, P. Potekhin, A. Tsvetkov, A. Vanin, V. Volkov, L. Voyevodov, V. Zhirnov, A. Zhuravlev*

Semiprecious Stone Carvers: *K. Ivanov, A. Kharlamov, A. Solovyev*

Semiprecious Stone Restoration Artists: *B. Igdalov, Yu. Molchanov, R. Shafeyev*

Scientific and Technical Support: *Yu. Alynin, D. Korablev, N. Onkasova (Zaikonnikova), S. Shadrin, V. Shchapov, S. Tuchinsky, B. Tyvrovsky*

Photographers: *A. Bugayev, V. Bugayev, A. Gorelik, B. Gorokhov, A. Minin*

The Amber Room has been recreated. A tremendous task that lasted a quarter of a century is completed. Undeniably our attitude towards this "double" of the lost masterpiece is inevitably ambiguous and the debates about the sense of carrying out this bold experiment in restoration will go on for many years. A very convincing answer to this question is provided in our opinion by the entire post-war history of restoration in our city during which many outstanding works of art have been returned from oblivion. It would be hard to find anyone today who would say that it was done in vain. More than twenty years ago, we took upon ourselves the immense responsibility for implementing a restoration project unparalleled in world practice. There followed years of intensive searching for the solution to incredibly complex problems, artistic, technical and financial. Yet at the same time those years were filled with a special meaning and relevance for those who were involved in the recreation of the Amber Room. Today we can state with satisfaction that thanks to this work Russia has acquired a unique school of restorers that revived lost crafts and technologies of the seventeenth and eighteenth centuries: artistic amber-working and the Florentine mosaic. The recreated Amber Room has already begun its life as a museum piece. And the activities of the Tsarskoye Selo Amber Workshop — to which the present publication is dedicated — have also become an inseparable part of the active, creative existence of our museum.

Ivan Sautov
Director of the Tsarskoye Selo
State Museum Preserve

For the renewal of the Winter Palace interiors after the terrible fire of 1837, Emperor Nicholas I ordered the coining of a medal bearing the words "Zeal overcomes all". Those words would provide a fitting epigraph for an event already achieved — the rebirth of the Amber Room — and a motto for work on the next project.

The recreation of a palace interior can be compared with a period play in the theatre: the restorers, like actors on the stage, need to live and breathe a different age in order to produce a unique work that has integrity. The show came off! The Amber Room staggers the imagination of everyone who enters the recreated interior. It is no easy matter to analyze the captivating breadth of feelings. You enter a special state, immersing yourself in an amazing world of amber whose energy was the secret knowledge of the Egyptian pharaohs and Ancient Rome.

In recreating the panels of the Amber Room and the Florentine mosaics the craftsmen revived and mastered new specialities that come down to us from the remote past. The principle that bound the work of today's expert restorers together in a single creative ensemble was virtuosity, many-sided methods of operating, the corresponding experience, an individual feeling for the material, a state of mind, keen eye and intuition. The team from the Tsarskoye Selo Amber Workshop saw the task through in one great burst of inspired enthusiasm. The creative process of reproducing the Amber Room revealed to us the lost skills of artistic amber-working and elevated the prestige of the St Petersburg school of scientific restoration, reviving the amber workshop that existed in Tsarskoye Selo in the eighteenth century.

Lara Bardovskaya
Chief Curator of the Tsarskoye Selo
State Museum Preserve

The recreation of the Amber Room is an event of immense historical and cultural significance that has attracted broad public attention. All the greater, then, was the sense of great responsibility and seriousness attaching to the task entrusted to us, and also the urge to "do one's utmost" as it says in one of the old documents about the Amber Room. The results of our efforts will be judged by many generations of visitors who come to the Tsarskoye Selo palace to see this "eighth wonder of the world" reborn. Behind us lay 24 years of endless tests, finds, bitter disappointments and happy discoveries, arguments and patient work, day in, day out. It is very hard to get accustomed to the idea that the greatest task of our professional lives has already been accomplished, that the best, brightest, most important thing that might occur in them already has. Not everyone managed to see it through to the end. But all those who at any time were involved in this unique restoration project deserve to be recalled with gratitude. When you understand what incredible labour went into this exquisite gossamer creation, it makes you want to acknowledge with warm sincerity people who were not just colleagues, but more like comrades-in-arms in a long and difficult adventure. Thanks to the restorers, architects and art historians, to all the specialists, with the aid of whose talent, knowledge and professional honesty we managed to resurrect and return to the public the appearance of one of art's legendary works — the Amber Room.

Boris Igadalov
Director of the Tsarskoye Selo
Amber Workshop public joint-stock company

Amber, as can easily be seen, is nothing but the sap of plants, since we sometimes find within it little animals and insects that were trapped in the once liquid sap... The rays of the low sun drove out this sap and the liquid dripped into the sea, from where storms carried it onto the opposite shore.

The Roman historian
Tacitus, 1st century A.D.

Introduction

The Heliades turning into poplars and their tears into amber. Illustration for Ovid's *Metamorphoses.* 1700s
Etching by Johann Ulrich Kraus

There are few today who know that the history of this "most remarkable stone of ancient times", as the great Russian mineralogist Alexander Fersman called it, goes back thousands of years. Its golden shine and warmth already captivated primitive human beings. Ancient peoples used legends to try to explain the mysterious origins of this unique gift of nature that embodies within it the warmth of the sun, the transparency of clear sea water and the scent of coniferous forests.

According to the myth recorded by the Roman poet Ovid, Phaeton, the son of Helios, the sun god, attempted to drive his father's chariot but could not control the fire-breathing horses and scorched the earth before plunging to his death. His mother and sisters (the Heliades) wept so sorrowfully over his grave that the gods took pity upon them, turning them into trees and their tears into golden amber.

In actual fact amber is the fossilized resin of coniferous trees and can be found in many countries around the world. The best amber, however, is gathered on the shores of the Baltic Sea.

It is there, on the coast of the Baltic, that the story of this unique creation of nature and human hands — the Amber Room — begins.

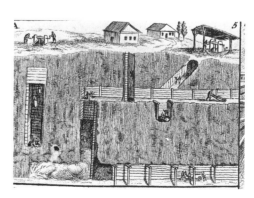

An Amber Mine. 1779
Etching by Johann Georg Penzel from a drawing by Johann Rudolf Schellenberg

9

A Short History of the Amber Room

View of the bay by the city of Danzig (Gdansk). 1730s–40s
Etching by Ginseppe Filosi

The seventeenth century was destined to go down as the Golden Age of amber-working in Europe. In that period East Prussia emerged as one of the foremost centres for the artistic treatment of the stone. The region possessed enormous reserves of the raw material, the collecting of which had been a state monopoly since the times when the Teutonic Knights held sway. The production of articles from amber was concentrated in the cities of Königsberg, Danzig, Lübeck and Elbing (now Elblag in Poland). The softness of the stone and the ease with which it could be worked — carved, turned, sawn, engraved and polished — meant it was used for a great variety of everyday articles for the wealthy inhabitants of Prussia. These were mainly small items: caskets, goblets, cups, vases, chess sets and jewellery. In the middle of the seventeenth century, though, a very important development took place in amber-working that would eventually make possible the creation of the Amber Room. The new technique became known as amber mosaic and required a wooden base to which thin sheets of amber, carefully matched together, were attached using an organic adhesive. This technique enabled the craftsmen to produce much larger objects, such as cabinets for studies. Sadly their magnificent creations had as a rule a very short life and needed constant maintenance. It turned out that wood and amber rebelled against such a close marriage as they react differently to environmental conditions. Many major experts on the history of artistic amber believe that the shift to the mosaic technique hastened the decline in the craft of amber-working. In the early eighteenth century, however, when the events that interest us took place, the craft was still full of vitality and immense creative potential. Frederick I, the founder of the Prussian royal dynasty, was remembered by contemporaries for his burning desire to outdo the sumptuous luxury of the French court. According to historical tradition, he liked the idea put forward by his court architect, Andreas Schlüter, to decorate a room in the Charlottenburg Palace outside Berlin with amber. As Schlüter envisaged it, the King's future study was to be completely lined with panels of amber backed with wood. Four large amber panels would contain large mirrors in elaborate frames in their centres. Smaller panels below would bear the Prussian eagle, a symbol of the state, and the monogram of Frederick I. The rich decoration of the interior combined relief carving of various kinds and extremely fine engraving backed by gold foil, fanciful patterns and complicated figurative compositions.

Design for three amber articles
1688. Workshop of Michael Redlin

A Jeweller's Workshop
Late 17th century. Engraving

*Portrait of Frederick I,
King of Prussia.* 1759
Etching and burin engraving
by Johann Ernst Gericke from
a drawing by G. Hempel

The creation of the amber decoration for the study began in 1701 under the direction of Gottfried Wolffram, a craftsman to the Danish royal court, and was continued in 1707 by Gottfried Turau and Ernst Schacht, amber-carvers from Danzig. Evidently while the work was going on, Frederick I decided that such a striking interior should be installed not in a suburban palace, but in his chief residence in the capital.

The amber panels were dismounted, taken to Berlin and set up in a corner room on the third storey of the royal palace. It must have been there that Peter the Great first saw the "amber wonder" when he visited Prussia in 1713 for talks with King Frederick William I, who had recently succeeded his father on the throne. The Russian Emperor left Prussia with the dazzling image of the Amber Study firmly in his mind and a burning desire to see the wonder in St Petersburg as the finest gem in his collection of curiosities.

This dream was destined to become a reality three years later when, after successful negotiations with the Prussian monarch, Peter was given "a most elegant present" —

*View of the Royal
Palace of Charlottenburg.* 1840s
Engraving on steel by E. Finden,
from a drawing by E. Gärtner

12

АНТАРНЫЙ КАБИНЕТ
Фридриха I в Берлине
Реконструкция
г. а. 1709-1711
№ 125

> Kedrinsky's graphic reconstruction
The detailed inventory that accompanied the amber panels when they were sent off to St Petersburg together with the study of historical photographs enabled the architect-restorer to establish the only possible arrangement of the panels lining the study of the Prussian King

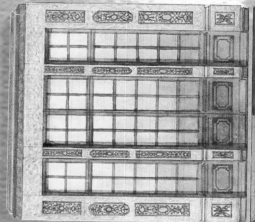

This is the image of the Amber Study of the King of Prussia provided by modern scholarly reconstruction based on the analysis of archive material. Sadly the fate of the actual designs for the study still remains unknown, which prevents positive identification of Schlüter as the author of this unique interior. How many agonizing problems could have been avoided, too, if the twentieth-century architects and restorers had had access to that priceless pictorial source material!

View of the Royal Palace in Berlin. 1799
Etching by Peter Haas, from a drawing
by Friedrich Calau

Portrait of Frederick William I,
King of Prussia. 1720s. Burin engraving
by Johann Georg Mentzel

the yacht Liburnica and the Amber Study. Frederick William who was noted for his exceptional miserliness and indifference to everything except warcraft and drill, had no regrets about parting with the study and relieving himself of the further expense required to finish it.

Although it was brought to Russia with great care in 1717, the Amber Study was never installed anywhere during Peter's lifetime. Evidently the reason was the lack of many details required to complete the decoration and the absence of experienced amber craftsmen. In the early eighteenth century this form of artistic activity was only just beginning to develop in Russia. For a quarter of a century the amber panels lay in their wooden crates in part of the Summer Palace complex, together with such exotic rarities as Dutch tiles and Chinese porcelain.

Peter's daughter Elizabeth recalled the Prussian King's gift after she herself came to the throne. The precious decoration of the study was ideally suited to the Empress's desire to have the interiors of her residence finished with unprecedented

14

Portrait of Peter the Great. 1845
Engraving on steel by an unknown
19th-century engraver, from an original
by Hyppolite Delaroche

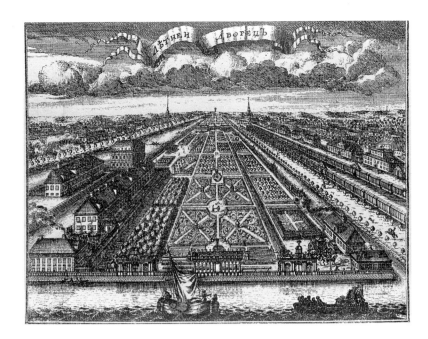

The Summer Palace
Engraving by Alexei Zubov
The palace had a two-storey service block (known as the Liudskiye pokoi) in the great hall of which the Amber Study was kept in dismantled form until 1743

splendour. Almost half a century after the magnificent room was conceived, it was made a reality, in modified form, by the great architect Bartolomeo Francesco Rastrelli whose work marked the highest point of the Russian Baroque style. Among his finest creations were the Winter Palace and the great palace at Tsarskoye Selo. It is with those architectural masterpieces that the further history of Frederick I's Amber Study is associated.

Empress Elizabeth gave instructions for the amber panels to be used to decorate one of the rooms in the (third) Winter Palace. Rastrelli had problems finding a suitable setting for the study and the panels were repeatedly taken down and moved from one room to another, until finally the choice settled on an antechamber adjoining the Empress's bed-chamber. The dimensions of this room were greater than those of the amber panels and so the architect was obliged to introduce lacquer painting imitating amber into the décor as well as eighteen mirror pilasters separating the amber panels.

Instead of mirrors, the opulent amber frames in the centres of the panels were filled with pictures "taken from the painter Grooth". Since the original decoration for Frederick I's study was never completed, one of the frames had to be made from wood. When he learnt about this, King Frederick II of Prussia made a gift in 1745 of a fourth amber frame. It was designed by Anton Rauch and incorporated allegorical elements extolling the Russian state. The restoration of the amber panels required after long years of storage and their installa-

Portrait of Bartolomeo Francesco Rastrelli Before 1762
Oil on canvas. Unknown artist
Hermitage, St Petersburg

РЕКОНСТРУКЦИЯ
1743 — 1755 гг.

A graphic reconstruction by A.A. Kedrinsky

Проспектъ пъ низъ по Невѣ рѣхѣ между зимнимъ
Ея Императорскаго Величества домомъ иАкадемiею Наукъ.

*View of the River Neva Downstream
between Her Imperial Majesty's Winter
Palace and the Academy of Sciences*
1750. Engraving by Mikhail Makhayev

Portrait of Empress Elizabeth. 1761
Etching and burin engraving by Yevgraf
Chemesov, from an original
by Pietro Rotari

tion in the palace was entrusted to Alessandro Martelli,
a specialist in plaster mouldings who had learnt how to work
with amber. For almost ten years the Amber Room was in the
Winter Palace, but this proved to be only a temporary stay.

In July 1755, when the Empress had resolved to have her
residence in the capital reconstructed once again, the amber
panels were taken down and sent to the great palace at
Tsarskoye Selo that would become the permanent home
of the Amber Room. In creating the Amber Room in Tsarskoye
Selo Rastrelli coped brilliantly with a very difficult task.
He had to fit the amber décor of a fairly small study into a
palatial state room with a high ceiling. Revealing a very subtle
talent as an interior decorator, he devised an alternating
arrangement of amber panels and mirror pilasters, murals
imitating amber on the upper part of the walls and sumptuous
gilded woodcarving. For all the opulence with which the hall

Vüe des bords de la Neva en descendant la riviere entre le Palais d' hyver de Sa Majesté Imperiale & les batimens de l'Academi des Sciences

was finished, everything surrounding the amber panels seemed a lightweight setting, underlying their fabulous beauty.

The main new element introduced into the rich décor of the room in Tsarskoye Selo was, however, the Florentine mosaics that replaced the paintings that had occupied the amber frames. These commesso compositions allegorically depicted the five senses: *Taste, Sight, Hearing* and *Touch and Smell* together. These pictures, made up of slices of semi-precious minerals fitted tightly together conveyed graphic detail and shades of colour with such precision that they gave the complete impression of easel paintings. The mosaics in the Amber Room were created in 1752 from cartoons by the artist Giuseppe Zocchi in the workshop in Florence run by the outstanding stonecutter and engraver Louis Siries. They almost certainly came to Russia as a diplomatic gift from the Austrian ruling house.

Frederick II, the Great, King of Prussia. 1746 Etching and burin engraving by Georg Friedrich Schmidt

Дворецъ Ея Императорскаго Величества въ Сарскомъ Селѣ XVI 22.5
въ 25 ти Верстахъ отъ Санктпетербурга.

*The Palace of Her Imperial Majesty
in Tsarskoye Selo.* 1755
Engraving by Mikhail Makhayev

Florentine mosaic: *Touch and Smell.* 1752
Louis Series, from the painted original
by Giuseppe Zocchi. Florence, Italy

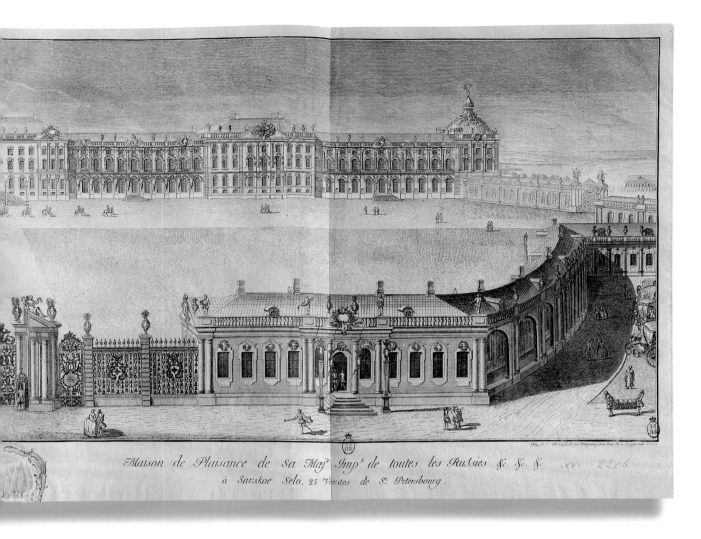

Maison de Plaisance de Sa Maj.t Imp.l de toutes les Russies &c. &c. &c. XVI 2216
à Sarskoe Selo, 25 Verstes de St. Petersbourg.

By December 1755 the decoration of the Amber Room in the great palace was in the main complete. Rastrelli described one of his own most original works in the following way: "*a large chamber entirely decorated with white and yellow amber and all the panels framed by carvings, decorated by bas-reliefs, festoons and other sculptural works in the same material. I gave orders for mirror pilasters with a pattern of gilded bronze to be placed between the panels.*"

Fifteen more years were needed, however, for this unique interior to acquire its final appearance. On one of the panels, amid the rocaille scrolls, you could find the inscription *Made in 1760 by Friedrich Roggenbuck, master craftsman.*

This inscription records the start of the final stage in the formation of the Amber Room. Its fragile décor required constant monitoring and maintenance. The specialist craftsman Friedrich Roggenbuck was invited from Prussia and given the post of curator of the unique interior for life. In 1761 several more Prussian amber-carvers came to assist

Cartouche with a mask from
the original decoration of the Study
of Fredrick I (after restoration)

Detail of the lower panel on the northern
wall of the Amber Room bearing Friedrich
Roggenbuck's autograph and the date 1760

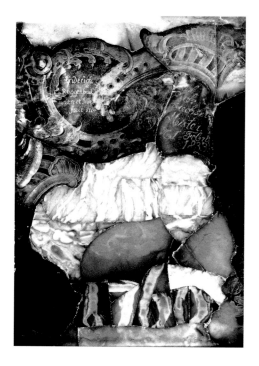

him, including his son Johann. In 1771 Johann succeeded his father in the post of curator, which he then held until his own death in the year 1813.

Under Friedrich Roggenbuck's direction additions were made to the amber decoration of the room: bases beneath the pilasters (previously these had been made of wood and painted in imitation of amber), eight smooth narrow strips of mosaic to fill the gaps between the pilasters, a corner console table, the composition above the eastern door and garlands at the tops of the walls. Those garlands incorporated masks that had been brought from Prussia together with the original panels and other amber details but with no indication of their intended location. As well as this, Roggenbuck introduced many embellishments to the original design of the wall panels. These include rocailles, flowers, cartouches, monograms of Empress Elizabeth and the double-headed Russian eagle in the decoration of the frame presented by Frederick the Great.

Only in 1770, when Catherine II had been on the throne for a number of years, did the seven-decades-long story of the creation of the Amber Room draw to a close. The appearance of this "eighth wonder of the world" astonished everyone who had occasion to visit the great palace at Tsarskoye Selo.

The French Romantic poet Théophile Gautier wrote with great enthusiasm: "Only in the *Arabian Nights* and

Portrait of Catherine II. 1762
Etching, mid-19th-century copy
of an original by Stefano Torelli

fabulous tales where the construction of palaces is entrusted
to sorcerers, spirits and genies, do people see halls of precious stones usually used for pieces of jewellery. The eye,
unaccustomed to seeing this material used on such a scale
is dazed and dazzled by the wealth and warmth of its shades
that represents the full range of yellows — from smoky topaz
to bright lemon..."

For almost two centuries the interior survived in Tsarskoye
Selo. In the course of several restorations (1833, 1893–97,
1933–35) carried out to the prevailing standard of the day,
losses, distortions and accretions inevitably took place
in the amber decoration of the room.

So, by the summer of 1941, when major restoration
work was planned for the Amber Room, it was already clear
that this was a work with a number of temporal layers
to it and that the restorers would be dealing with a highly
complex artistic organism. The outbreak of war on June 22
killed all the creative plans. Ahead lay the occupation of
Pushkin (Tsarskoye Selo), the removal of the Amber Room
to Königsberg and its subsequent mysterious disappearance.

Only forty years later would restorers again turn their
attention to the Amber Room, but now they were faced with
an immeasurably more difficult, responsible and unprecedented task — the recreation of a lost masterpiece of world
culture.

The stone-cutter N.G. Petrov mounting
details in one of the narrow panels

The Rebirth of the Amber Room

Hundreds of articles, dozens of books and many years in the lives of serious investigators and adventurous treasure-seekers have been devoted to the search for the Amber Room. With every passing year that separates us from the moment when the "eighth wonder of the world" disappeared, the hope of it returning again grows ever dimmer. If the famous Amber Room were being kept secretly in a private collection, over half a century some sort of hint about the fate of such a well known work should have leaked out to collectors, museum workers or journalists. And if the crates containing the panels still remain in some underground hiding place, the fragile amber decoration that even before the war was in urgent need of restoration will literally crumble apart in the hands of its happy discoverers. And even if the amber panels have somehow been kept in the best of conditions, the scale of the losses will be so great that after conservation work they will have to be displayed as individual elements in the decoration of an irreparably lost artistic ensemble that once was the Amber Room.

М.Г. Воронов, А.М. Кучумов

ЯНТАРНАЯ КОМНАТА

ШЕДЕВРЫ
декоративно-прикладного
[...]а из янтаря

ПОХИТИТЕЛИ ШЕДЕВРОВ

Во время второй мировой войны немецко-фашистские захватчики подвергли варварскому разграблению оккупированные территории европейских стран. В частности, из Советского Союза и Польши гитлеровцы под предлогом «обеспечения сохранности» вывезли многие художественные ценности, составляющие национальное культурное достояние. С этой целью были созданы даже специальные подразделения, как, например, «айнзацштаб Розенберга», о мародерских операциях которого рассказывается в публикуемой статье. Эшелонами вывозились в «рейх» музейные коллекции, библиотеки, архивы, ценнейшие произведения искусства, многие из которых не найдены до сих пор.

Эккерт КЛЕССМАНН

«ЦАЙТ-МАГАЦИН», ГАМБУРГ.

B се это напоминает детективный роман, с той только разницей.

славился своими ками. В начале новил Штайн, ко конфискованы вла целью использован Сюда стали прибы ные составы из «в В последние месяц ждению Штайна, в глубине 660 метров содержимое 24 ваг два больших ящика янтаря» из Кенигсбе тинского университе вили в феврале 1945

Может ли идти ре комнате, учитывая, чт действительно было ц янтаря? Да, уверяет новное доказательство включается в телеграм 16 января 1945 года рер СС Отто Рингель Кенигсберга в Берлин. В ное содержание: «Янтар Операция завершена. Об щен в Б. Ш.» В доку

КАК НЕМЕЦКО-ФАШИСТСКИЕ ОККУПАНТЫ
ПОХИЩАЛИ НАЦИОНАЛЬНЫЕ ХУДОЖЕСТВЕН
ЦЕННОСТИ ДРУГИХ НАРОДОВ

следы затерялись там же. С

ПО СЛЕДАМ ЯНТАРНОЙ КОМНАТЫ

Карл-Хайнц ЯНСЕН

«ЦАЙТ», ГАМБУРГ.

T уристы из ФРГ заполнили анфилады комнат Екатерининского дворца — летней резиденции царской семьи в Пушкине, бывшем Царском Селе.

— А сейчас, — возвышает голос экскурсовод, — мы находимся в Янтарной комнате.

Потолочная роспись комнаты восстановлена, но стены голые, не считая одинокого фрагмента отделки из матово-блестящего янтаря, призванного показать, как прекрасно будет выглядеть комната после завершения реставрационных работ.

— Великолепная обшивка стен вместе с зеркалами пропала во время войны, — больше экскурсовод не сообщает.

— Не иначе, какой-нибудь генерал прикарманил, — сострил один из туристов, не подозревая, насколько близок он к истине.

Когда в январе дям открылась был были разрушены и ревья. Потребовало сяцев оккупации. В их исках сообщает зап

крепости Бойен. «Восточ началом А. Розенберга, в дать ее украшением и с году, однако, про гауляйт

ВИТАЛИЙ АКСЕНОВ
ДЕЛО О ЯНТАРНОЙ КОМНАТЕ

ДОСЬЕ

ЗР 1-85

Рига, 1979, 24 июн

РИГАС БАЛСС. Суббота, 23 июня 1979 года

репортаж

порога Янтарной комнаты

на свете найдется, которые ниче... бы о знаменитой комнате короля Фридриха, Петру I. уникальную ...во-Пушкино. бесследно Великой по... оккупу

нимаются будущие железнодо... рожники.

Лет десять назад мне впервые пришла в голову мысль попробовать восстановить Янтарную комнату, — рассказывает Блинов-старший. — К ее осуществлению я готовился все эти годы. Изучал историю, архитектуру, историю искусств, механику, историю ... Жесконечно могут знать рые

тами нашей работы ознакомились представители Дирекции дворцов, музеев и парков рода Пушкина и Всероссийского общества охраны памятников истории и культуры и дали им положительную оценку.

— Сколько же требуется

в оригинале. Сохранивши снимки Янтарной большого ложительную оценку. ...но по качестве

Detail of the recreated overdoor
composition (*dessus-de-porte*)
Restoration artist A.K. Kochuyev

Ceiling painting: *The Marriage of Chronos*
Recreated from a sketch by an unknown
18th-century artist from the Hermitage
collection. A team of restoration
artists led by Ya.A. Kazakov

Meanwhile in the late 1950s restoration of the Catherine
(Great) Palace in Tsarskoye Selo began after the destruction
and looting of the war years. The work included the "Golden
Enfilade", Rastrelli's suite of state rooms, the chief attraction
of which was the Amber Room. Originally it was decided
to recreate its painted decoration, gilded carving and elaborate parquet floor, in other words, all the elements of the
interior, except the amber panels. It was proposed to cover
the places where they should have been with fabric.

At that time the recovery of the original decoration of the
Amber Room seemed highly probable. Besides, in those post-
war years the remarkable cultural phenomenon that is the
Leningrad school of scientific restoration was only just
beginning to form. Decades of painstaking labour in bringing
back to life first-rate works of painting, sculpture, architec-
ture and applied art would be needed before the very idea
of recreating such a unique masterpiece as the Amber Room
ceased to seem absurd.

It was, however, hard to come to terms with the thought
that future generations would never be able to see the
fascinating, fabulous beauty of the Amber Room. It was
unpleasant, too, to think that the once magnificent art
of amber-working had declined in our own time to the level
of undistinguished mass production.

In the late 1970s a group of craftsmen led by the architect
Genrikh Khazatsky was given the task of designing a new
museum of amber in the city of Kaliningrad (the former
Königsberg). Naturally the culmination of a history of artistic
amber-working was to be a display devoted to the Amber
Room. The artists prepared a one-fifth scale model and
several fragments of the décor of the lost interior . This work,
which earned the approval of Grigory Romanov, the head
of the Leningrad Communist Party organization, enabled him

Detail of the Décor
Second half of the 19th century
Watercolour by P. Grekhnev

to approach the Soviet government with a proposal
to support an initiative for the recreation of the legendary
Amber Room. A well-argued justification of why the question
was being raised and a detailed plan of the work required
enabled Khazatsky's group to obtain a historic positive
decision.

On 10 April 1979 a government resolution marked the
beginning of what has been perhaps the boldest experiment
in the field of restoration worldwide — the recreation of the
Amber Room. The restorers had at their disposal only a black-
and-white photographic record of the amber panels,
a single pre-war colour slide showing the room, a single
watercolour by the artist c, reproducing a detail including the
monogram of the Prussian King, and some
fifty small fragments of the amber decoration: parts of mouldings, carving and the flat mosaic. The task of reproducing the
amber panels on the basis of such material seemed just too
fantastic.

There was, however, also a unique collection of amber
articles saved during the war years and returned to the Catherine Palace from evacuation. These pieces were direct analogies
of the Amber Room: in terms of time and place of creation,

The only colour slide depicting
the original Amber Room. 1910s

Casket. 1705. Gottfried Turau, Danzig
The State Tsarskoye Selo Museum Preserve
*In 1983, when the casket was being
restored, the signature of Gottfried Turau,
one of the creators of the Amber Study
of Frederick I, was discovered on it*

style, methods of working the amber, and — in one instance —
even authorship, indicated by the signature of Gottfried Turau.
It was with the study, restoration and copying of this collection
of seventeenth- and eighteenth-century works that the team
for the recreation of the Amber Room began its activities.

In 1981 their workshop became part of the research and
production association called *Restavrator* (Restorer), while
the artist and experienced stone-cutter A.A. Zhuravlev
became its head. His energy and enthusiasm made it possible
to successfully tackle an extremely difficult set of problems
at the initial stage of the recreation project. With him from
the outset were the stone-carver A. Vanin and the architect-
stone-cutter A.A. Krylov who was destined to pursue the
many-year course of recreating the Amber Room to its end.

The future restorers already had an artistic education
behind them, as well as experience in jewellery, stone-cutting
and sculptural work at the *Russkiye Samotsvety* and *Rosmon-
umentiskusstvo* works. Still, they needed several years
of working with the amber articles in the collection in order
to master the forgotten technology by which they were
made and to understand the aesthetics prevailing in the
plastic arts in the relevant era. Without that, there was a great
danger that they would produce a cold, intellectual copy
devoid of the inner dynamism, immediacy and vivid feeling
that are so much a part of Baroque art.

At work recreating the Amber Room
*On the left in the foreground
is A.A. Zhyravlev, artistic director
of the workshop from 1981 to 1997*

M.G. Kolotov, historian and art expert

The question of how precisely the copy would correspond to the lost original was one that art historians and architects working for the Tsarskoye Selo museum preserve and *Restavrator* had to resolve over two decades. Their painstaking research work made it possible to determine the make-up of the original décor of the study in Berlin, to establish the time when later additions appeared, to trace the provenance of the Florentine mosaics and to find analogies for lost details. For those two decades the overall scholarly direction of the historical researches devoted to recreating the interior was in the hands of M.G. Kolotov, one of the most authoritative art historians working in the field of restoration.

It emerged in the course of the investigations that the famous Tsarskoye Selo interior was never recorded in technical drawings, engravings, paintings or graphic art (with the exception of one watercolour).

Hence the main primary sources on which the restorers could base their work were the photographs. Eighty-six photographs of the interior were traced in the Hermitage, Russian Museum, Tretyakov Gallery and various archives. They began with the first picture, published in 1859, and ended with the ones taken when the room was in Königsberg castle.

33

The central panel on the southern wall
of the Amber Room. 1902
Photograph

>The northern wall of the Amber Room.
The mosaic picture *Sight* in an amber
frame. 1910s photograph

In 1986 Yu.V. Trubinov carefully systematized all the available photographic record of the Amber Room, compiling a comprehensive catalogue with a detailed description of each shot.

After the photographs were all rendered to a common scale, the team managed to obtain a picture of the general view of the interior, to establish the exact dimensions of the amber panels and their decorative elements. Certain details of the panels could not be made out even with a magnifying-glass as they were hidden beneath a thick layer of lacquer. In that event the team either consulted forensic experts, who had special photographic equipment at their disposal, or drew on historical descriptions and the analogies provided by amber articles in museum collections.

After an analysis of the material gathered by researchers on the creation and subsequent history of the Amber Room it was possible to say that a scientific reconstruction of the lost work was feasible, with the details unrecorded in any documentary source being reproduced through the use of analogies. The volume and quality of the historical evidence available to the restorers provided a sound basis for the recreation of each detail and, consequently, for the production of an extremely reliable artistic image of the work that was to be reborn.

The results of the scholarly researches lay behind the project for the recreation of the Amber Room drawn up by a group of architects headed by A.A. Kedrinsky. That outstanding professional restorer, brilliantly knowledgeable

A.A. Kedrinsky, chief architect
of the Amber Room recreation project

Colour standards for the amber panels

and practically experienced, devoted a considerable part
of his life to brining back the ensembles of Tsarskoye Selo.
Kedrinsky and his assistants (N.P. Ivanov, Ye.I. Korovina,
Ye.I. Volkova. M.N. Kononova, N. Lobantseva, V.V. Lipatova,
Ye.N. Skryleva and I.V. Yarotskaya) chose the long and
difficult course of scientific reconstruction, that is to say
the pursuit of maximum fidelity to the original appearance
of the Amber Room. The process of producing a drawing
of the entire composition of the interior involved scrupu-
lously tracing from the old photographs the exact shape
of each flat piece of amber and three-dimensional element.
The later insertions made during unskilful refurbishments
were detected. The elements that were missing or insuffi-
ciently visible on the photographs were designed anew
on the basis of analogies, the reliability of which was thor-
oughly grounded by the researchers. The project for the
recreation of the Amber Room included six volumes of work-

The workshop of Kedrinsky's
architectural group

ing drawings, full views of the walls, standardized colour scales, designs for the parquet floor and ceiling painting. It was complete in the main by the autumn of 1986.

The most important part of the project was to be full-scale designs for all the amber panels. The process of producing standardized colour scales and depicting the amber decoration in all its multiplicity of colour brought to the fore the problem of establishing the colour scheme from black-and-white photographs. The planners had at their disposal only one colour slide, a watercolour depicting part of a lower panel and the working documents from the pre-war restoration in which the arrangement of the stones was analyzed. In view of the obvious inadequacy of this material, the team had to resort to a very unusual and ingenious method of getting round the problem. They took black-and-white pictures of surviving fragments of the original décor of the Amber Room, details of articles in the Tsarskoye Selo collec-

Northern wall

Eastern wall

"*The amber panels were the product of a complex synthesis of several art forms. Their appearance was founded upon the superbly drawn general architectural composition for lining the walls of the interior. The ornamental sculpture, three-dimensional edging and the texture of the surface belonged to the realm of plastic art, while the extremely rich gradations of colour across the entire surface can be regarded as decorative painting. The uniting together of all three art forms in one work, combined with the superbly brought out decorative qualities of the 'sunny stone', is what made the artistic image of the Amber Room*".

A.A. Kedrinsky

Southern wall

Western wall

Project for the recreation of the Amber Room

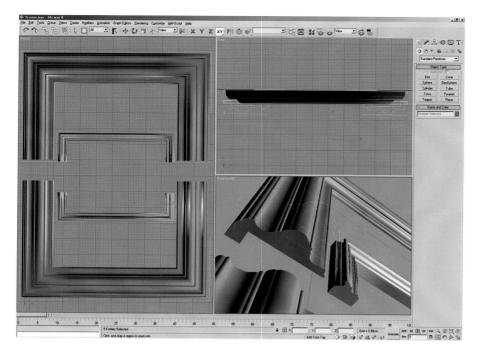

Determining the cross-section of the large amber frame using computer modelling

tion and pieces of amber of various shades. By comparing the photographs they managed to establish the colour scheme of the amber panels with a sufficient degree of accuracy. The authentic works in the Catherine Palace collection were a further aid to determining the use of colour characteristic for the period in question.

Another of the difficult problems at both the planning and implementation stages was determining the height of the amber relief carving from photographs giving only a flat image. This was surmounted by a unique method of photogrammetry developed by the All-Russian Scientific Research Institute for Mine Engineering and Surveying. Using special stereogrammetric cameras to view the old photographs it proved possible to determine the outline dimensions and shape of a lost detail. As the years went by, however, new methods of determining the parameters of elaborately shaped details became available that were based on the latest computer technology.

At the same time as the design was being produced, the long process of finding and mastering the techniques required for restoration work was underway. Amber is a soft, but at the same time very fragile material and so the creation of elaborately shaped details required a special tool that no-one had ever used before. One of the most experienced restorers, V.M. Domrachev who had a background in both art and technology, developed special milling cutters with ten and twelve cutting edges. These cutters looking like metal flowers were produced at the Voskov Tool Factory in Sestroretsk outside Leningrad. The workshop was gradually equipped with lathes and milling machines adapted in speed and method of operation to the specific properties of amber. For fine handwork gravers and other tools were acquired or specially produced.

A fair amount of time needed to be spent too on new developments that would ensure a long life for the recreated amber décor.

The restorers knew that sheets of oak had been used as a base to which the flat pieces of amber and relief details were attached. That variety of wood, however, is particularly hydroscopic and consequently reacts strongly to changes in temperature and humidity by changing its geometrical dimensions. As a result all the history of the completed Amber Room was accounts of sticking pieces of amber back into the places from which they had fallen. With the aid of a manufacturer *(Nauchfanprom)* various types of plywood were tested, with the sort used in the aviation industry eventually coming out on top.

The mastic (in the foreground) used in mounting the amber pieces

The choice of mastic with which to attach the amber to its backing was no easy one either. It needed to meet several requirements at once: not to harm the amber, to give firm, yet not permanent adhesion — in other words to leave the possibility of removing an amber detail from the board should it require restoration. Analyses of samples of authentic mastic taken from amber articles were carried out with the aid of specialists from the Central Leningrad Research Laboratory. More than 100 cycles of such testing were carried out, recording the effect on the mastics of changes in temperature, humidity and ultraviolet radiation. The ideal options turned out to be wax-resin and wax-gum damar mastics in which natural beeswax purified of mechanical inclusions was used.

Last but not least, the main technical problem for the recreation of the Amber Room was the colour scheme of the interior. Archive sources and

Applying the mastic to the wooden base before fixing the pieces of amber

The process of colouring the amber
The restorer A.A. Krylov

literature failed to provide information about the way the amber was coloured when the decoration was being created. Study of the surviving fragments of the Amber Room was not sufficient to reach a definite conclusion about the dye-stuffs employed, as certain organic compounds responsible for colour are present in the stone itself. A long and sometimes acrid debate began among specialists over the advisability of artificially colouring the amber. Some expressed fears that thermal methods of colouring would cause damage to the surface of the amber, as it begins to oxidize when heated to temperatures above 50 degrees Celsius. It remained to be hoped that natural aging would over the centuries give the amber the desired strength of colour.

However, the natural varieties of Baltic amber have a fairly narrow range of colours, while the Amber Room was celebrated for its rich chromatic palette, including shades from bright lemon to wine red. It was known that the practice of colouring amber went back many centuries. Pliny the Elder already noted that the craftsmen of Ancient Rome altered the colour of amber using the plant alkanet *(anchusa tinctoria),* Tyrian purple and goat fat. According to German eighteenth-century encyclopaedias, in the 1720s the dying of amber was still well known. The study of original items in the laboratory of the Hermitage showed that in two cases out of three Baltic amber had been tinted. The clear amber was subjected to thermal treatment, while the opaque (bastard) stone was tinted using special pigments of natural origin. It emerged that such treatment did not invest the amber with alien properties, but only expanded its chromatic possibilities. But what temperature and what pigments could be used on the amber without causing damage? These questions would be studied in four St Petersburg laboratories: at the Technological Institute, the Earth's Crust Research Institute, the *Restavrator* association and the Hermitage. Their efforts resulted in the development for the first time in the field of jewellery and restoration of a technology for colouring amber with synthetic pigments.

Detail of a historical photograph
of the mosaic picture *Sight*

Recreated fragment of the mosaic
The Port in Leghorn

One of the key elements in the decoration of the Amber Room was the four colourful mosaics made of natural minerals. When they began work on them, the restorers had only black-and-white photographs , pre-war descriptions and the comment in Alexander Benois's work on Tsarskoye Selo asserting that the compositions were taken from paintings by Giovanni Paolo Panini. Investigation into the provenance of the mosaics was made necessary by the pressing need to obtain information about their colour scheme and the minerals used. A serendipitous find enabled the researchers LV. Khaikina and M.G. Kolotov to establish the name of the true author of the painted cartoons and the survival of those cartoons in the museum of the Florentine workshop in which the mosaic pictures in the Amber Room had been made. This success made possible the creation of colour standards for the works to be recreated. A signifi-

44

Cartoon for the mosaic *Sight*. 1751. Giuseppe Zocchi
Museum of the *Opificio Pietre Dure*, Florence

cant factor, too, was the existence in the Tsarskoye Selo
museum collection of another Florentine mosaic — *The
Port of Leghorn* — produced by the same craftsmen as the
Five Senses in the Amber Room. The forensic laboratory
made an analysis of a scraping of mastic from that mosaic.

To try out his hand and develop his technique the stone-
cutter Boris Igdalov reproduced part of the *Port of Leghorn*
mosaic measuring four centimetres by seven. That small
fragment was made up of over a hundred pieces of semi-
precious stone, each of which provided a barely detectable
nuance of colour, the transition of tone and a fanciful
curvature of line. It took three months to produce this test
piece, while the reproduction of the four mosaic pictures
for the Amber Room, each measuring 56 centimetres by
43, would take several years. The realization of this unique
labour of love required the collection of raw material,

Reconstructed detail
of the mosaic picture *Sight*

45

7

8

9

10

6

5

4

3

2

1

11   12   13

14

Minerals used to recreate the mosaics

1. *Urals jasper*
2. *Revno jasper from the Altai*
3. *Lapis lazuli from Transbaikalia*
4. *Nephrite from Transbaikalia*
5. *Lapis lazuli from Transbaikalia*
6. *Urals jasper*
7. *Urals jasper*
8. *Nephrite from Transbaikalia*
9. *Urals jasper*
10. *Urals jasper*

11. *Urals jasper*
12. *Flint from the Moscow region*
13. *Urals jasper*
14. *Urals jasper*
15. *Urals jasper*
16. *Urals jasper*
17. *Flint from the Pamir mountains*
18. *Flint from the Moscow region*
19. *Onyx from Pakistan (not shown)*

15

16

17

18

The mosaic picture *Touch and Smell*
An authentic part of the decoration
of the Amber Room discovered
in Germany in 1997

The restoration stone-cutters
R.N. Shafeyev and B.E. Mints

minerals, from right across the former Soviet Union. The restorers engaged in recreating the Florentine mosaics — Igadalov, R. Shafeyev, Yu. Molchanov, A. Solovyev and K. Ivanov — found themselves faced with a real test of their professional skills. The discovery in Germany in 1997 of one of the authentic mosaics, evidently looted during the removal of the panels from Tsarskoye Selo, provided specialists with a rare opportunity to compare a newly-recreated work with the original. They proved almost indistinguishable! And this fact, it seems to us, is sufficient to put an end to the debate on the correctness of the decision taken over twenty years ago on the possibility of "repeating the unrepeatable" — reproducing the Amber Room.

The finishing of this unique interior involved all the techniques used in artistic amber-working: flat mosaic setting, three-dimensional and intaglio carving. The flat mosaic that

The mosaic picture
Touch and Smell

Top: The original painted cartoon
1751 Detail

Centre: The authentic mosaic
Detail

Bottom: The recreated mosaic
Detail

makes up the smooth surfaces of the panels consists of small sheets of opaque amber five millimetres thick. They are polished, cut *en cabochon* (with a slightly convex top) and carefully fitted to each other. The broad expanses of polished slices create the impression of a single honey-gold mass. The transparent sheets are embellished with fine engraving like those images that cause us to look with intent admiration

Detail of the recreated amber facing of the panels (flat mosaic)

Fitting together elements of the amber mosaic

50

at the amber boxes and caskets of centuries past.
The intaglio carving is carried out on the reverse side
of a clear piece of amber. This requires virtuoso skills on
the part of the craftsman and a jeweller-fine design applied
to the stone with the aid of a microscope. The fast, precise
cutter carves the amber into seascapes and fanciful
ornamental compositions that seem transfused with glowing
light. This effect is achieved by backing the sheets of amber
with gilt foil.

The finest amber is used for three-dimensional carving.
Whole nodules or composite pieces are used for multi-figure
compositions, garlands, pictures, acanthus leaves and other

The restorer N.V. Mazur engraving on amber

Examples of internal carving
on the medallions of the corner panels
(above and left)

51

The plaster modeller
Yekaterina Anokhina at work

details. This is the most difficult form of carving, requiring a highly qualified exponent. There is a great danger of making an error in proportions, the height of the relief or the character of the element. For that reason sculptors produced preliminary plaster models of the decorative details, recreating the aesthetic world of the eighteenth century: Bible characters, the gods of Olympus, playful cupids and whimsical rocaille scrolls.

The plaster casts were handed over to the most experienced and skilled amber-carvers, looked up to with respect by their younger colleagues. In their many years of work on the recreation of the Amber Room, the restorers

The large amber frame on the eastern
wall of the Amber Room. Plasticine model
by Ye.N. Anokhina and Yu. V. Anokhin

A production meeting
The restorers S.P. Kaminsky,
Yu.A. Fedoriak, V.V. Kurakin, B.P. Igdalov
(workshop director), A.M. Krylov,
architects A.A. Kedrinsky, I.V. Yarotskaya
and the restorer V.M. Domrachev

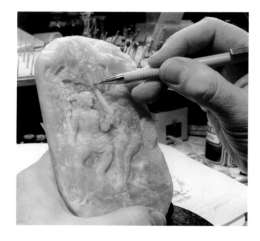

Amber carvers at work

A.M. Krylov, V.M. Domrachev, S.P. Kamimsky, V.I. Mezentsev, V.N. Gundarov and others managed to combine total immersion in the style and spirit of an age long-past with a very high degree of creative freedom that enabled them to avoid the obvious coldness and dryness of a copied work. Yet at the same time, in order to totally exclude the possibility of artistic arbitrariness in the process of reproducing the original, the craftsmen's work was constantly and fastidiously monitored by one of the project's authors — the architect I.V. Yarotskaya.

At the final stage of work on an amber panel, all its elements were polished, pierced and temporarily mounted using a special mastic. After this preliminary assembly, the amber was tinted and only then were all the carved details finally attached to the wooden base and fitted tightly together to leave no gaps. The finished panel would be mounted in its historical position in the Amber Room and the craftsman would remember the day as one of the most outstanding in his professional life. After each piece of the décor had been recreated, it was presented for approval to a panel of experts that included researchers and senior administrators of the

54

Tsarskoye Selo Museum Preserve as well as major specialists in the field of applied art and restoration from the Hermitage and the State Inspectorate for the Preservation of Monuments.

For two decades the invariable supplier of raw material for the reconstruction project was the Kaliningrad Amber Group of Enterprises — the largest enterprise exploiting the region's unique deposits of amber. The restorers had to carefully select pieces of the stone to find the right kind, size and pattern for the recreation of a particular element of the decoration. Provisional estimates suggest that some six tons of amber was required to realize the entire project. Even during the most difficult days of Russia's recent history, the work on the recreation of the Amber Room still continued thanks to the efforts of the administration of State Tsarskoye Selo Museum Preserve. The management did everything possible to support the workshop, while the leadership of the team itself had to make great efforts so as not to lose first-rate restorers with priceless experience. From 6 September 1999, the completion of the project was financed by the German company *Ruhrgas*. Thus, like its predecessor, the new Amber Room linked together the two countries, Russia and Germany.

Culminating moments in the recreation of a figure of Neptune, the god of the sea, and his invariable attribute the trident

55

< The Amber Room in the Catherine
(Great) Palace at Tsarskoye Selo
The final stage of the restoration

The reborn interior in Tsarskoye Selo is unarguably
a product of the twentieth century as well as the eighteenth,
demonstrating the mutual links and continuity between
the cultures of various eras and nations. Visitors to the Amber
Room can enjoy the captivating play of colour in this unique
interior and the boundless fantasy of Rastrelli, and also, of
course, admire the selfless labour of the people who worked
to recreate this masterpiece.

The Amber Room Resurrected

< The door in the south wall
of the Amber Room

Gilded bronze wall-light, part
of the decoration of the Amber Room

Carved decoration around the door
in the south wall of the Amber Room
(from above)

<< The art historian M.G. Kolotov
and Alexander Kedrinsky, the author
of the project for the recreation of the
Amber Room, in the resurrected interior
May 2003

Details of the upper tier of decoration in the Amber Room. Painting on canvas in imitation of amber mosaic, woodcarving and gilding.

The ceiling painting
and upper tier of decoration
on the walls of the Amber Room

David and Saul
Engraving from the book
Teatrum Biblicum Tabulis, 1614
Amsterdam

Details of the decoration
on the amber frame on the north
wall of the Amber Room:
a composition with military
attributes and the bas-relief
David and Saul (above);
the Russian imperial crown and
monogram of Empress Elizabeth
(below)

> The large amber frame
on the north wall of the Amber
room

Moses and Aaron before Pharaoh
Engraving from the book
Teatrum Biblicum Tabulis, 1614
Amsterdam

< Bas-relief of *Moses and Aaron
before Pharaoh*

> Bas-relief of *The Healing
of the Syrian General Naaman*

Details of the decoration on the large
amber frame on the north wall of the
Amber room (pages 70–73)

< Detail of the amber facing (flat mosaic)

The corner panel on the south wall
of the Amber Room

Medallion with internal carving

Pedestal of a pilaster on the north wall
of the Amber Room

> Details of the decoration
of the lower tier of panels: a heraldic
composition featuring the Prussian
coat of arms and the monogram
of Frederick I

< The large amber
frame on the south
wall of the Amber
Room

The Russian
imperial crown

Details of the decoration of the large amber frame
on the south wall of the Amber Room

< A sculpture of the goddess of victory

> The coat of arms of the Russian Empire

Mosaic pictures in the Amber Room that allegorically depict
the five senses: *Touch and Smell, Hearing, Sight* and *Taste* with some details

The stone-cutter B. Mezentsev at work

The Tsarskoye Selo Amber Workshop Today

Tsarskoye Selo (the town of Pushkin)
The service wing of the Catherine Palace
that houses the Tsarskoye Selo
Amber Workshop

Icon of The Adoration of the Magi
19th century. Mother-of-pearl, and wood
The Moscow Kremlin State Museum
Preserve

A small wing of the Catherine Palace in Tsarskoye Selo houses a workshop in which artistic stone-cutters work. Here, just like a couple of centuries ago, they create with affection, concentration and unhurried care articles from a unique natural material – amber, reviving the venerable traditions of an exalted craft as well as a belief in the exceptional artistic potential of the stone from the Baltic.

In two decades of work on the recreation of the famous Amber Room, the Tsarskoye Selo Amber Workshop became one of the world's most significant centres for the study, restoration and reconstruction of works made of amber and semiprecious stones. Through many years of research the workshop developed a method that on the one hand allowed the team to come as close as possible to the historical techniques originally used to produce the items being restored or recreated, while on the other ensuring a long future life for them. This approach is unparalleled inside Russia and abroad.

Working within the creative workshop are restoration artists who have earned the highest possible qualifications. They are capable of carrying out the most complex tasks in restoring, recreating and copying the finest examples of amber work and the artistic use of semiprecious stones from centuries past. The skilled hands of these experts have

Card table. 18th century
Constantinople. Mother-of-pearl, gold,
tortoiseshell, copper. The Tsarskoye Selo
State Museum Preserve

Mantel clock. 1860s
Felix Chopin factory, St Petersburg
Bronze, copper, enamel. The Tsarskoye Selo
State Museum Preserve

restored a large group of amber items from the collection
of the Tsarskoye Selo State Museum Preserve. At the request
of the Armoury Chamber in Moscow, the workshop restored
silver-trimmed marble tables from the seventeenth century,
as well as a nineteenth-century icon inlaid with mother-of-
pearl in a wooden case. The St Isaac's Cathedral museum
collection in St Petersburg contains nineteenth-century
examples of Florentine and Roman mosaics (tabletops,
clocks, a plaque) restored by our craftsmen.

For the Kaliningrad Museum of Amber, the workshop
is carrying out the scientific reconstruction of items from
the "Königsberg Collection" — one of the finest European
collections of artistic amber that was lost during the Second
World War.

The restoration practices of the Tsarskoye Selo Amber
Workshop have attracted the attention of foreign specialists
in the field of decorative and applied art. Representatives
of the workshop were invited to restore an eighteenth-century
casket from the Museum of Amber in Varde, Denmark,
an amber altar from Schloss Kopining, Germany, amber
archaeological artefacts kept in the National Museum, Bel-
grade, Serbia and a Urals malachite fireplace set from a private
British collection.

Fire screen. 1860s.
Peterhof Lapidary Works, St Petersburg.
Designed by Ippolito Monighetti. Lapis
lazuli, gilded bronze, silk. The Tsarskoye
Selo State Museum Preserve

Map of the World. 2001. Amber, wood, gilded foil. Relief carving, engraving and tinting. Produced by a group of craftsmen led by A.M. Krylov at the Tsarskoye Selo Amber Workshop. The image is based on a map created in the 1720s by the Nuremberg cartographer and geographer Johann Baptist Homann

Icon of Saints Boris and Gleb. 1990s
Amber, wood, gilded foil. One of the
series produced by the Tsarskoye Selo
Amber Workshop for the residence
of the President of Russia in the Kremlin

The workshop also produces unique original works. These include an eighteenth-century geographic map reproduced in amber and individual elements in the furnishing of a ship's cabin for the display of the Museum of the World Ocean in Kaliningrad. Among the workshop's most significant works is a series of seven icons produced using the Florentine mosaic technique and amber to decorate the residence of the President of Russia in the Kremlin, as well as diplomatic gifts for the German Chancellor, the King of Spain, the Patriarch of All the Russias, and other distinguished figures.

The regular products of the workshop differ radically from mass-produced items in the use of an incomparably larger

The shop of the Tsarskoye Selo Amber Workshop

range of techniques for the working of amber and semi-precious stone. The high aesthetic qualities of the items created by the restoration craftsmen can be judged by visitors to the shop that the workshop has recently opened. The team is also engaged in the design of clothing embellished with amber.

The Tsarskoye Selo Amber Workshop actively involves itself in publishing and exhibition work. It has great experience of participating in international exhibitions held in the USA, Germany, Denmark, Japan, Finland and other countries.

The workshop's many and varied artistic activities are testimony to the immense creative potential of this unique enterprise that has revived the lofty traditions of European stone-cutting art from centuries past.

Sculpture of Saint Jodocus (Judoc). 2000
Created by N. Petrov at the Tsarskoye Selo Amber
Workshop. A reconstruction of a 17th-century item
from the Königsberg Collection that was lost
during the Second World War

95

Front row
(seated, left to right)
Yu. Fedoriak
I. Mezentseva
V. Gundarov
A. Kharlamov
M. Kolotov
A. Kedrinsky
O. Murashov
N. Mazur
I. Zagorny
A. Bashmakov
V. Kurakin

Second row
(left to right)
M. Trufanova
A. Minin
B. Igdalov
A. Konoplev
V. Mezentsev
L. Khaikina
N. Akhtulov
R. Voyevodov
I. Yarotskaya
V. Domrachev
S. Kaminsky

T. Nechipurenko	V. Miasnikov
L. Vilde	T. Makarova
I. Pustoshnaya	K. Senchuk
V. Novikov	O. Semenchenko
Ye. Anokhina	L. Voyevodov
O. Melnikova	V. Demenkova
R. Shafeyev	
V. Alimov	**Third row**
S. Ilyin	**(left to right)**
A. Krylov	G. Budiakov
N. Belitsky	V. Verigin
B. Mints	A. Dogadin
Yu. Molchanov	A. Murzov

> *Clock. 1995*
Amber, mother-of-pearl, gilded foil, metal. Created by A. Krylov at the Tsarskoye Selo Amber Workshop. A reconstruction of an item from the Königsberg Collection that was lost during the Second World War

Casket. 1990s
Amber, wood, gilded foil
Produced by N. Petrov
at the Tsarskoye Selo Amber workshop to a design by
M. Kononov

Casket. Late 17th century North Germany
Amber, ivory, wood, metal
The Tsarskoye Selo State Museum Preserve. Restored by A. Krylov at the Tsarskoye Selo Amber Workshop in the 1990s

Casket. 1999
Replica of an 18th-century work
From the collection of the Tsarskoye Selo State Museum Preserve
Created by V. Domrachev at the Tsarskoye Selo Amber Workshop

Bowl. 1998. Amber and metal
Created by V. Domrachev at the Tsarskoye Selo Amber Workshop
A reconstruction of an item from the Königsberg Collection
that was lost during the Second World War.

Goblet and Candlestick. 2001
Amber and metal. Created by A. Vanin at the
Tsarskoye Selo Amber Workshop. A reconstruction
of items from the Königsberg Collection that was
lost during the Second World War

< *The Coat of Arms of St Petersburg
in the Second Half of the Nineteenth Century.* 2003
Amber and wood. Produced by the Tsarskoye
Selo Amber Workshop for the 300th anniversary
of St Petersburg as a gift for President Putin
of Russia and Chancellor Schröder of Germany

< *Altar*. 1990s. Amber, wood, metal
Replica of an 18th-century work
Created by N. Petrov at the Tsarskoye Selo Amber Workshop

Icon of The Saviour. 2002. Amber, wood, gilded foil
Created by S. Ilyin at the Tsarskoye Selo Amber Workshop

< *Crucifixion.* 1990s
Amber, ivory, metal, gilded foil, wood
Created by A. Krylov at the Tsarskoye Selo
Amber Workshop. A reconstruction
of an 18th-century item

Sculpture of A Moorish. *Boy with Fruit.*
2002. Obsidian, jasper, metal. Created
by R. Shafeyev at the Tsarskoye Selo
Amber Workshop

Florentine mosaic plaques. 2001–02
Created by R. Shafaeyev, Yu. Molchanov
and A. Kharlamov at the Tsarskoye Selo Amber Workshop

> *Sculpture of A Peasant with a Samovar.* 2001
Jasper, metal. Created by R. Shafaeyev
at the Tsarskoye Selo Amber Workshop

< Battle on the Ice chesspieces. 2002
Amber and metal. Designed and
created by V. Karnaukhov at the
Tsarskoye Selo Amber Workshop

Chess set. 1990s
Replica of an 18th-century work
Amber, wood, gilded foil. Created
by A. Vanin at the Tsarskoye Selo
Amber Workshop

>> *Amber jewellery*
From the clothing collection. Designer
T. Chernova, amber carver V. Domrachev

ЯНТАРНАЯ КОМНАТА
ВТОРОЕ РОЖДЕНИЕ
(на английском языке)

Издательство «Альфа-Колор», Санкт-Петербург
Тел./факс (812) 326-8384 E-mail: alfac@wplus.net